The Sun Rises in the North

THE SUN RISES
IN THE NORTH

Debjani Chatterjee
John Lyons
Cheryl Martin
Lemn Sissay

Smith/Doorstop Books

Published 1991 by
Smith/Doorstop Books
The Poetry Business
51 Byram Arcade
Huddersfield HD1 1ND

ISBN 1 869961 32 3

British Library Cataloguing-in-Publication Data
A catalogue record for this book is available from the British
Library

Typeset at The Poetry Business
Printed by Tri-Com, Birstall, West Yorkshire

The Poetry Business gratefully acknowledges the financial assistance of
Yorkshire Arts, Kirklees Cultural Services and North West Arts.

CONTENTS

FOREWORD

'Black poets', 'women poets', 'Northern poets' — the labels are slick, but sometimes they seem to diminish the writers to whom they are attached. The virture of *The Sun Rises in the North* is that it is a collection of poems which, by any standard, is work of quality. These are poets fullstop. They do not ask to be judged by special pleading or seek preferential treatment through a process more of social engineering than artistic opinion.

In magazines or at public readings I have encountered the work of Debjani Chatterjee, John Lyons, Cheryl Martin and Lemn Sissay before this anthology, but I am delighted to see their poems gathered together representatively and with enough of each to whet my appetite for whole collections by all of them. Each of these is an expert reader of their own verse. There is no use pretending that on the page their vocal inflections or their performing style can be captured completely, though people who have heard them give their work aloud will hear in their minds their distinctive orature qualities. 'Doing the Dog' by Cheryl has a humour which nevertheless comes across without us needing to hear it. The conversational epistolary flow Debjani's 'Writing to Comfort Nehru's Daughter' works equally well when read aloud, as letters sometimes are, or read in solitary silence. John Lyon's poems have a tenderness and Lemn Sissay's an energy which communicate as fully on the page as they do out loud.

I am honoured to introduce these poems to you. The North of England should be proud to have such writers bred in its soil and scenting its air. A new generation of poets is declaring itself, and the four poets in this collection are up there with its best.

Alastair Niven
Director of Literature, Arts Council of Great Britain.

Debjani Chatterjee

DEBJANI CHATTERJEE was born in India, and has lived in Japan, Bangladesh, Hong Kong, Egypt and Morocco. She is now Director of the Sheffield Racial Equality Council.

Her first full collection, *I Was That Woman*, was published by Hippopotamus Press in 1989, and her second is due from Enitharmon Press in 1992. Other books include *The Role of Religion in A Passage to India* (Writers Workshop Press, Calcutta) and *The Elephant-Headed God & Other Hindu Tales* (Lutterworth) which was selected for Children's Books of the Year 1990. She has co-edited a bi-lingual anthology of prose and poetry, *Barbed Lines* (Bengali Women's Support Group & Yorkshire Arts Circus), which won the Raymond Williams Community Publishing Prize 1990.

She has been a winner in the Lancaster Literature Festival Open Poetry Competition and the Peterloo Poets Poetry Competition (Afro-Caribbean/Asian Prize).

Arrival

The cardinal winds have brought us here,
Now battered, now buoyant, we survived.
What mattered most was getting it clear:
no longer strangers, we have arrived.

Fair Weather

(an English-as-a-Foreign-Language poem)

Hello friend! I am friendly, yes?
'Is fair weather'? Yes, very much:
sun is equal not-so-hot on all,
rain is ever on you, and me also ever,
cold is very much on all also.
English friend ever talk weather.
I come from sunshine very much –
I not like fair weather, so talk weather never.

Paolozzi's Magic Kingdom

You just enter it and suddenly – you're lost.
No, don't expect to spend a pleasant afternoon:
you won't idle away an hour or two munching
a lazy sandwich, yawning a cup of tea,
glazing at the décor propping up in symmetry
the usual pillars of commercial artistry.
Throw away the price tags of Harrods and Sotheby's.
Didn't the publicity warn you this exhibition
was fiendishly combined to split your mind?

Bite on the bullets of memory, tossed,
pelletted unremittingly with a loving obsession,
again and again, plundered and lost.
This bin kingdom is a magic wasteland
presided over by a skeleton jangling
on a key chain, shorn of dignity and sham;
a rubbish dump overrun by flies, cockroaches, snails,
spiders, scorpions, copulating crickets and butterflies,
where tawdry frogs on cracked mirrors croak fairy tales.
This nightmare catalogues
all that is lost and all that is found;
the power of hidden springing surprises,
the toymaker, child, primeval artist,
the sculptor, scientist, magpie, rag-and-bones man,
the savage who is hunter, arch sorcerer, death's head,
out of context, out of time, objects
that are subjects of a strange affinity,
skulls, and weapons civilised,
dredged from aboriginal resources –

the fake reality cheek by jowl with the reality of fakes.

Nothing lives or dies in this kingdom,
but is metamorphosed, cannibalised.
The accoutrements of cultures, centuries and fetishes
press down, stratified with mud and humour,
a lick of paint, a flick of glitter,
history pitfalled with follies,
sermons of silly profundities,
white man's burden, black man's inheritance
of this kingdom of magic and waste
recorded on camera, displayed,
entered in a little black notebook labelled
Eduardo Paolozzi, a secret diary with cuttings
of newspaper peeping between leaves.
Essence is captured in scraps of wood,
fragments of cloth, a seed pod,
basketry, pottery, machinery, nuts and bolts,
cogs and wheels, ropes and braids, bulbs and beads,
the flotsam of humanity washes composite faces,
and the human hand engages to grab
while muted music plays on warrior pipes.

And as you leave, one line anonymous
comments on postcards, may not go amiss.
Deposit them anywhere, your distilled emergences
for new audiences from east and west
to comment on your lost and found rapport,
like a vast undying conga flowing in and out
of this magic kingdom.

Writing to Comfort Nehru's Daughter

Hindi did not come easy,
a hard and hybrid alien.
It was not her mother tongue.

So it was the national
language. Nothing to do with
quality or richness, but
everything with politics.

No sweet reverberations
of so much Indian speech.
Where was the dry brilliance
of English scattered like dust?

Even *Chacha* Nehru lent
such grace to the medium
which gave insight to *Glimpses*,
access to *Discovery*.

She laboured, disgusted, through
extra coaching, oppressive
essay assignments, Kabir's
dohas duly memorised
without study, alphabets
daily butchered in orgy.

Then Nehru was murdered. Schools
and offices closed. No time
for heated language riots.
Grief communicates itself,
though tortuous its channel.

She set herself the task of
writing to comfort Nehru's
daughter in *rashtra bhasha*.
Childish, but panascopic.
Hindi did not come easy,
a hard and hybrid alien.

Towers of Silence

When we were classmates, I told you my dreams, Homi:
dreams of Juliet against a London sky,
a matchmaking umbrella sheltering us,
even though it never rained in my dreams.
You clapped my back on Chowpatty beach
as we threaded our way through hawkers and pyedogs.
I was the one with an eye to the future,
but you always kept your head:
'Come to the pictures, *yaar*,' you'd say,
'and Aunty Mehroo's for a top class *chaat*.'
Campus life was an oasis which nourished
the branching of our separate ways.

Your letters are most solicitous; I sense
the happy marriage – product of careful planning
by family and friends, the steady grooming
of the business you partner with your uncle;
I picture the comfortable middle aged spread,
not that the studio photograph shows it;
is your top balding, I wonder? Mine is.
You have landed on your feet.
I took off as I always knew I must –
I suppose I won some measure of success.
You ask about my dreams. In truth, Homi,
I don't remember them in the mornings.
But I know they are of home, for I awake each day
to the boisterous din of Bombay's traffic
raining echoes on a Docklands tenement.

Of course there are Parsees here. Past masters
at immigration, we know all about integration.
Our clubs are here and there. But back home
the towers of silence are calling me.

Bhai Karim Afzal

Bhai Karim Afzal,
in childhood our worlds met:
we collected crickets and pigeon feathers,
I set my sights on music and song,
you spoke casually of medicine
being in your blood and bones.
One wall stood between us
and we played in courtyards under one sky.
We hopped back and forth between roof tops;
and the benign peepal tree,
demolishing garden boundaries,
was a passport to shared domains.
Today miles and years later,
We are India and Pakistan.

Bhai Karim Afzal,
nearest to that brother I never had,
I missed you when my family moved away.
When chance returned us to the old house again,
we were teenagers – tongue-tied.
Then I caught you one day in the garden:
absorbed,
knife bared –
blood – pain – twisted things
I recognised as frogs dissected,
more jars lined up
for the slaughter of experiment
in the secret corner where our friendship bloomed.
We gazed in an anguish of dismay
and rushed away in guilty sentiment.

Today miles and years later,
we are India and Pakistan.
You are a scientist in a provincial town
and I juggle between poetry and prose.
Between here and there, by chance
our different orbits met.
We were shy strangers,
loving regret between us.
Bhai Karim Afzal,
nearest to that brother I never had,
I miss you.

Making Waves

Newsflash: 'Britain's no longer an island.'
The ears pricked up at the late night telly.
Only connect to this sceptred isle, land
Of European solidarity.
Eurospeak is now the lingua franca.
The year rushes to link with a new one
Of wall to wall breaking perestroika
And Channel Tunnel digging to '91.

Linked to Europe, we're linked to Africa,
To Asia. So welcome, Britain, to the world!
A night for counting Welsh sheep barbequeued
Beside a Euro butter mountain.
Morning: a flooding sea of commuters
Bursting from the station. Hadn't they heard?
But each one travelled with stiff upper lip
Bridges drawn up as they wade through the waves.

The Sneezeeling

Third cousin twice removed to the Raja of Johore,
Jester extraordinaire to rulers of Mysore,
Ambassador designate at court in Bangalore,
Is the celebrated Sneezeeling of Singapore.
His manners are so jolly, his folly's so profound,
His anecdotes and silly quotes on all sides astound.
Rubies dangle from his ears with diamonds commonplace,
As he sits and schemes and sneezes, smiles adorn his face.
He bows and scrapes and pirouettes, dainty on his toes,
A spectacular legend, a man who has no foes.
This amazing Oriental dazzles with his charm,
His blunders are forgiven, he 'never means no harm!'
The Sneezeeling is Singapore's celebrated seer.
From Macao to Mangalore the world won't see his peer.

In the Republic of the Blind

In the republic of the blind
you are the one-eyed,
        three-eyed
                omniscient king.
You are everywhere, but I
who neglect the *pujaroom*
notice you in the toilet
        and bedroom
                in discomfiture.
Benevolent Big Brother,
you are not an Englishman
– you don't understand about
privacy. Gentle, you are
        no gentleman.
You hang about like lovers,
        like muggers.
                at corners
of dark streets. You rip me up.
No day passes that you are
not by me, sitting on the slip
of a moment's epiphany
to remind me that I have not
committed myself to you.

My feelings are shamelessly wrapped
about you, they throb hot and cold.
But my mind is promiscuous
and my actions pointless.
I run but roads everywhere crawl
in your domain and direction.
Why write your endless *lila*, Lord,
wasted on those who cannot read?
I do not even know my need
– Paradise well lost to poets
without vision beyond the pale.
But you wait to guide my wayward
hand to the alphabet in braille.

Traffic

The traffic moves as traffic always does
– bar accidents.
We meet, we smile, we say 'hello'
– maybe.
Should we stop and for how long?
Shall we discuss the weather
or have we graduated from that
to higher or more intimate things?
How are you today?
I feel disposed to unbend a little
and tell you that you must visit us
– someday.
Are we ready to exchange confidences?
I hate those yellow shoelaces
– are you colour blind?

Did he pass by and incline his head?
Now what could that have meant?
Did her mouth curve upwards
and was there recognition in her eyes?
No, we did not hold each other
for more than a split second
– if that.

On a winter's day we walked by,
wrapped in fog and convention.
We each waited on the other
– except that we did not wait.
In a cool politeness that did nothing
to thaw the day,
relieved of the necessity
of acknowledgement,
cheated of the burden
of conversation,
vaguely dissatisfied,
we would not halt the traffic.
The traffic moves as traffic always does
– bar accidents.

Patrimony

'Demand your patrimony,' Mother said.
'Your father approaches. The moment's here!'
Her expression bitter, age lined her eyes.
Like destiny the crowd of monks grew near:
every hand held a beggar's bowl, every
head was shaved. She looked at, but did not see;
she could not, would not, point him out to me.

'A prince's first-born can ask anything
of his father. Someday you will be king.
Stake your claim. After long years he has come.'
I searched a saffron sea – each serene face.
The one with the confident stride drew me.

'I am called Rahul of the Sakya race.
Father, give me my due,' I insisted,
tugging hard at the lean monk's robe. 'Where
is my inheritance?' Mother's gaze now
was luminous, the stranger's full of care.

He handed me his empty bowl and looked
at her he'd left behind. He raised one hand
in showering blessing. 'Son, join our band,'
he said, begging forgiveness all the while.

His radiant face mirrored Mother's smile.

Sultana Razziya
I

'Sultana Razziya zindabad!'
The crowds shouted themselves hoarse
when none but you were left
between the throne and anarchy.

Long years ago, Iltutmish, your father,
had the wisdom-folly dictated
by desperation to name you his heir.
'We have always placed the sultanate
above all other interests,' he told
the silent surly noblemen. 'We did not
subdue Bengal, Bihar and Sind; crush
rebellions; avert the catastrophe
of Mongol hordes overrunning the land;
consolidate our empire; only
to have it all vanish like some desert
mirage in the next generation.'

'Sons were sons,' the durbar murmured.
But your sire knew all about ability.
Finger raised in admonition, he could
acknowledge the incompetence of sons:
'Remember Aram Shah, our brother-in-law,
great Qutb-ud-Din's disasterous progeny.
You yourselves begged us to bring an army
out of Baduan to rid you of this dynasty.
Our sons too are of that ruinous ilk.'

Only Iltutmish could have the audacity
and vision to name you a leader of men,
he likened your razor sharp mind to that
of blessed Ayesha. When a 'Slave of a Slave'
could occupy Delhi's peacock throne,
one could begin to contemplate
a mere daughter succeeding him.

All agreed, but when your father died, history
repeated itself – and your discretion lay
in waiting – it was Rukn-ud-Din Firoz
they raised and suffered, then deposed,
as your father's ghost watched him flounder

under the burdens of state. Chaos reigned,
till at last the mob cheered you heartfelt:
'Sultana Razziya zindabad!'

II

'Sultana Razziya zindabad!'
For the good of the many, in your father's name,
for the sake of the sultanate . . .
'She is her father's daughter!'
they praised. But what did that mean?
You knew that you were your own woman.

The crown adorned your curling locks,
crest of peacock feathers eyeing the multitude.
You did not want this, gently born,
what did you care for rule and power?
Yet leadership became you, you knew
where your duty lay, all your life you had
breathed the hot-house air of court intrigue.
You would grow into the job, you told yourself,
be the very model of a Muslim queen,
the flower of Indian womanhood.
When the court painter petitioned you
for sittings, you dispensed with the customary
lotus and rose, but posed in quarter profile,
your henna-patterned hands holding a drawn
sword – a delicious curve like Cupid's bow –
perhaps the artist saw beyond you.

You smiled at your cheering subjects,
promised them unity, protection, glory, peace.
The pillared halls echoed with lusty cries:
'Sultana Razziya zindabad!'

But almost at once the murmuring began:
'ruling a sultanate was no easy task
and women were ever frail, it was unnatural
to stay single at her age and the Sultana
needed the guidance of a man.'
Conspiracies were hatched, divisions emerged,
the powerful muscled their way to your presence,
bent on wedding power, power that lay with you.
But you were your own mistress now
and sent the sniffing wolfhounds packing,
though they waited at the gates, tongues lolling.

'We will not be ruled by a woman,' they said.
'Let us see how she copes in battle.'
Revolt spread like forest fires and each one
taxed you more than the last to stamp out.
You learnt to win some over with honeyed words,
others you had to fight, all had to be kept at bay.
Your glamourous figure riding with the troops
was hailed with shouts and some unease:
'Sultana Razziya zindabad!'

III

But was this seemly, was this natural?
Every question returned to the basic one
of the rightness of a woman ruling alone
over civilised Muslim men. The Prime Minister
had much to say on the obscenity of your position.
His pastime was the writing of secret letters
and constant quoting from the Quran in conversation –
funny how often the subject was women!
Your duty lay in marriage, he said;
you should give the people what they were used to –
a sultan. But you were wilful.
Razziya, gently born, would have wed
some royal suitor at her father's bidding.
But Sultana Razziya would rule her own destiny.

By dint of ability, and with his master's example
beckoning, Iltutmish had risen from slave
to Governor to Sultan and, along the way,
had married the Sultan's daughter.
You, Sultana, favoured an Abyssinian slave.
When a man aspires, it is admired;
When a woman stoops, she is beneath forgiveness.

Open rebellion flared up: governors,
once your suitors, now waged war.
It could not last. No one was ready
for the phenomenon of a Muslim queen.
Though you paved the way for so many
Mughal wives to rule after you,
they did so from behind the purdah.
You led your soldiers into battle,
but they would not be led. Captured,
imprisoned, days numbered, you reflected on
the fickle kismet that led you here, to shouts of:
'Sultana Razziya murdabad!'

NOTES

Writing to Comfort Nehru's Daughter p.14
Chacha: Hindi word meaning Uncle. Nehru was *Chacha* Nehru to children all over India where his birthday is celebrated as Children's Day.
Glimpses: Nehru wrote *Glimpses of World History* for his daughter, Indira, while he was in prison.
Discovery: Nehru's *The Discovery of India* is a classic of Indo-Anglian literature.
Kabir: North Indian mystic who tried to reconcile Muslims and Hindus. His *dohas* or prayers are famous for their devotional quality.
Rashtra bhasha: national language, *i.e.* Hindi.

Towers of Silence p.15
Yaar: pal
Chaat: a dish of spicy mixed fruit
Parsees: Zoroastrians descended from the Persians who fled to India from Muslim persecution in the 7th and 8th centuries. Under the British Raj, Parsees took to British education and adopted some British ways. They concentrated in Bombay which developed into the commercial centre of western India. Parsees have excelled in commerce and trade, travelling to many business capitals around the world. Parsees dispose of their dead by leaving them on their 'towers of silence'.

Bhai Karim Afzal p.16
Bhai: brother
Karim: one of Allah's names, it is an Arabic word meaning 'merciful'.
Afzal: Urdu derivation from the Arabic 'Afdal' meaning 'the best', it is one of Allah's names.
Peepal: a tree sacred to Hindus who will not cut it. Walls and buildings can be destroyed if it grows too near them.

In the Republic of the Blind p.19
Pujaroom: prayer-room. A traditional Hindu home always has a *pujaroom*.
Lila: divine play. According to a Hindu belief, all of creation is God's *lila*.

Patrimony p.21
Rahul: son of the Buddha and Yashoda, at fifteen he followed his father's example and joined the Sangha, the brotherhood of Buddhist monks.
Sakya: the Buddha's clan.

Sultana Razziya p.22
Sultana Razziya: talented daughter of Iltutmish, she ruled from 1236 to 1240 AD.
Zindabad: long live!
Murdabad: death to!
Iltutmish: a slave of Qutb-ud-Din Aibak, he won his master's favour and was elevated to Governor of Baduan. Later he replaced Qutb-ud-Din's son, Aram Shah, to become sultan (1211 − 1236 AD). Since Qutb-ud-Din also rose from slave to sultan, Iltutmish was called 'Slave of a Slave'. Although he appointed his daughter Razzia to succeed him, two of his sons had brief spells as sultan: Rukn-ud-Din Firoz after Iltutmish died and Nasir-ud-Din Mahmud a few years after Razziya was put to death by her nobles.
Qutb-ud-Din: founder of the Slave Dynasty, he ruled the Delhi Sultanate from 1206 to 1210 AD.
Ayesha: favourite wife of the Prophet Muhammed and a respected commentator on the Quran and the Hadith.

John Lyons

JOHN LYONS was born in Trinidad, and has lived and worked in Manchester since 1967.

His collection *Lure of the Cascadura* was published by Bogle l'Ouverture in 1989. He is represented in several anthologies, including *New British Poetry* (Paladin 1989). He has won the Peterloo Poets Afro-Caribbean Poetry Prize twice as outright winner (1987 & 1991) and once as shared second winner (1988). In 1991 he was awarded an Arts Council Literature Bursary.

As a painter he has exhibited both nationally and internationally. He has been a purchaser for the Arts Council Art Collection.

No Apples in Eden

There were no apples in Eden,
only sapodillas ripening among
bougainvillaea and frangipani.

The serpent was a mapepire snake
in the sapodilla tree, observing
how God drugged Eve with deep sleep,
plucked an organ from her body,
fashioned it into Adam.

This snake with guile in smooth slithers
curled around Adam's thighs, stirred his desires,
sweetened his tongue with words
as delicate as the flavour of sapodillas,
made a seducer of him.

And when Eve uttered Adam's name
at the acme of her pleasures,
Eden shook under God's footsteps.

Oh the discovery of shame!
They covered their nakedness
with blooms of bougainvillaea.
The mapepire hid in a balisier flower.

Ma Trojidah

She startled the sun-scrubbed
city-day of Port-of-Spain
when she walked out of a sepia photograph
taken by a 'Massa' proud of his chattel
in the heyday of sugarcane.

Her long 'twelaylay' patterned frock
conjured up these islands' history:
pungent sweat odours of labouring in troubled earth,
stench-thickened darkness in ships' holds,
the despair of barracoons.

In this attire, a century out of fashion,
she prodded unavailingly colonial consciences
for signs of guilt.

Birth of Carnival

Long after burning cane fields,
it was freedom time to fashion
features of Europe: Jabmolassie and his:
'Pam palam pam pam,
    pam palam pam pam.'

The carnival of the French
eclipsed into hiding, a private affair.

And the drumming, no longer the beat
of feet on the plantation roads
rushing to douse cane fires.

Attempts were made to stop
'flambeaux'-lit 'Camboulay'
Troops came out.
Man-o-wars rode
the oily undulating sea
in Port-of-Spain harbour.

Myth Maker

For this green water fowl
every ochreous dry season
is ritual death in this scorched gully.

Yet, a wet season ago
it was a green flash splash – landing
in deepest water where the gully bends;

or in its spindled strut
disturbing the shallow pools' stillness,
coiled spring of its neck wound back
to strike at guppy and crayfish.

Its death is a stink now,
rising from feather-bag of bones;
but life will flesh it up again
for another wet season.

Where Aspirations Wilt

In wet seasons and the whisperings
of worlds teeming under damp leaves,
weeds aspire to bloom amidst the elected maize;

but comes the ritual drought,
and the sun fills its days burning up
their will to emulate the poppies' glory.

In these yellow-ochry, Caribbean summers,
the air is a sharp intake of breath
held between burnished brass sky
and the tension of dust waiting
to be stirred up at the least provocation.

You can smell the heat;
odours of seared flesh;
feel the land's shock
under the sun's hammering.

There is nothing for it but acquiescence
in overpopulated shadows, and dreams of wet seasons.
Still, the maize dries well for grinding.

Bobolee

Good Friday,
like holy Granma Sundays.

Baptist shouters in long white cotton
walked like in funerals,
ringing bells,
singing hymns.

We waited for hen to cackle.
When we found her egg
we put the white in a drinking glass,
left it in Good Friday sun,
watched our future appear in pictures;

then the Judas rag doll,
as big as a man,
was dragged through the streets.

Every beating boy with a long stick,
'bolee, bolee, beat the bobolee,
bolee, bolee, beat the bobolee',
beating towards the big fire waiting
for Judas in the stone quarry.

Aiyo! Aiyo!

I saw him purse his lips,
heard him whistle a breeze for flying.

In the answering gust
I lifted from his quivering thread of fist.

Sun-proud in orange and yellow,
I serpentined to an eagle height,
razor-zwilled tail of blades
and slivers of green glass
lust-glinting to dive, to cut loose
my nearest enemy.

And when I dived
my tail was a thread-slasher;

aiyo! aiyo!
to the enemy's dying drift
towards tangled green graves
of faded kites.

At Antoine's Barber Shop

There was a time, swivelled to its full height,
I still needed a wooden box in the barber's chair.

I was growing to the decreasing swivel of a man:
'If only yuh dead mudder could see you now,' Antoine said.

I listened to the rapid scissor talk and barber shop debate:
'Man, Sugar Ray could box fuh so!
He better than your Joe Louis, any day.
I tellin yuh, HE was a sweet sweet mover.
Joe Louis flat-footed, cahn dance like ole Sugar.'

And when the razor came out unfolded,
slapping itself keen on the leather strap,
I held my breath, stopped listening
till soap suds were wiped away.

'Brilliantined', talc-powdered,
unscathed with short back and sides,
I left the barber shop shadow boxing.

Flying a Bunting for Manhood

By some strange coincidence
Reverend Cumberbatch chose
Corinthians one, verse eleven
for his Sunday preaching text:

'When I was a child, I spoke like a child
. . . when I became a man, I gave up
childish ways.'

That day of all days,
with me proud as a young yard cock
in my first long pants.

That day I held my nose high,
higher than when I found my first secret fob.

Fists deep in side pockets,
nobody could call me mannish.

With impunity I was able to hang a hankie
from my back pocket, flying like a bunting.

There was manly substance about me
in those long pants styled like Rochester's.

That Sunday night my father, a little embarrassed,
gave me a book covered with brown paper;
'A book every young man should read,' he said.

Grown Away

When I was a 'shirt-tail' runaway,
trailing in the current of my speed
a brown paper 'chikee-chong' kite,
giddy as a butterfly,

time was long, long;
time was a day of marbles
in clean-sweep yard-ground,
'stick-em-up' among 'pillar-trees' under house,
where the dry, dry dirt was dust bath for fowl.

Sometimes we told jumbie stories
in the moonlight on back door steps,
sitting close-up like chickens
perched in a fowl-run for sleep.

But all that was some time ago,
before the balisier flower
hatched for the nation a mapepire zananna
with a franchise like a sting.

In England now, I ask myself,
does Dolan Corner jumbie still haunt
the blind bend under the tamarind tree?

Moving On

We live inconsolable days
where rain like tears veils near hills,
alters our perception of striving.

Some days go beyond wind of change
when fury of hurricane smothers our cries.
Nevertheless, we move on
clinging to precipitous ways
pioneered by maroons.

So many struggled this way before us,
churned up mud with their urgency.
On these slippery slopes
feats of our forefathers
are toe-holds in our climb
to yet another summit,

a panoramic perspective
of our future hazed with uncertainties,
Babylon not yet in sight;
but we move on.

Tellin Stories

Teacher mus tink
I am a chupidie;
she tellin me bout cow
jumpin over de moon.

Dat is mamaguy.
I wonder how
a cow could jump so high!

But dat not de only lie!
How bout dis dish
dat run way wid a spoon.

I expect dat soon
she go talk bout some fish
in shirt and tie
talking to a snail
bout somebody steppin
on he tail.

King Top

Every little shirt-tail vagabon know in Lavantie
Neville guava wood top is king top;

but Winston want to show he better than he,
didn't buy no top from Ole Hezikiah shop,
instead, he chop a piece wood from soursop tree.

With Great-granma cutlass he shape it good;
scrape it and scrape it till it smood, smood.
Then he hammer in a six-inch nail;

he got so excited, he open he mout an he shout:
'Crapaud smoke yuh pipe dis time widout fail,
mister Neville. I go shut yuh big mout,
den yuh go know wat I talking bout.'

Eventually when Neville met Winston, Neville said,
'Hey, Winston, I hear yuh mek new top
from soursop tree jus so yuh could challenge me.'

Well, Winston give Neville a cut-eye, cheups at he.
'Bet yuh life, mout'er, meh new top is king top now,
put yuh blasted top on de groun, I go show yuh how.'

Neville draw a line on the road with he king top;
'nearest dis line mus have first go.
Believe me, Winston, today I go mek you a pappyshow.'

Winston he went quiet quiet winin up the marlin
on he top, gettin ready to spin.

Nobody breathin. You could hear a pin
drop on de ground. He point he top to the line.
He raise he top-han in de air
an, 'VVVUP'; Winston was grinning from here to ear:
his top come right down on de line, steady as a rock.

It was hummin like a hummingbird an spinnin sweet.
Well, Neville, he mout wide open, he full ah shock.

'Winston,' he said, 'I jus remember, I ehn tellin lie,
is meh Granny, she sen me to de shop to buy
a poun ah saltfish, ochra an sweet potato,
see yuh fuh now, we ketch up tomorrow.'

Kind Thoughts a Stripper

We allowed her our back yard
to play in. It was a game she played
alone with her child's used nappies.

We recognised her darkness
from a long way off, knew its intent;
constructed as swift as a spell
barriers of kind thoughts.

We watched her thin pretences fall away.
Her nakedness scared the dog,
attracted the devil's magpie.

Drinking up the Drizzle

What is there to be done
but stare astonished at the greyness
swallowing up a weaker relation
of my tropical sun!

I take the unbelievable stance:
stoic expressions,
– no efficacy in home-spun philosophy –
'my spirits must drink up the drizzle'.

But there is no obeahman here
to push the Pennines away,
or turn the wind about.

Cheryl Martin

CHERYL MARTIN was born in Washington DC. She has lived in England since 1983 when she came to study at Emmanuel College, Cambridge. She is currently finishing her PhD at Manchester University.

She won the Cultureworld English Poetry Prize in 1990, and in 1991 One Step Theatre Company produced her first British play, *Late Night Ice Cream*. She also works with Pit Prop Theatre in Leigh. She won an Arts Council Resident Playwright Award, and a Northwest Playwrights Resident Writer grant for 1991-92.

She sings jazz with the Oscar Cheerful Band and in the duo Fine and Mellow.

A Stone-Selfish Son-of-a-Bitch Has Picked Me Up And Dropped Me Blues

Yet another man
I thought I could trust
has done his best
to thrust me into misery.
So what's new? Honey,
I've walked this road
before. And more-
over, on the way
I've been spit on
by the same
spotted toads.

Paradigm

Christ
must have been
a woman.

Sweet Bird of Youth, the Nightingale

Night settles on my skin, a thousand flies.
In the mirror a younger woman's face, unmarked.
No trace of pain, even under the eyes,
or of locked wards, medicine that wouldn't work,
blood in the bath, stomach-pumps, amphetamine wires,
razors, burns, bile, scars –
mad heart like a Maserati –
gone. I live in silence.
Pills, removal vans, packing.
Sounds of lips cracking.

I have been ill, Mother;
my life lost
in lusty destruction: savaged,
in love with a snowman
who confuses freezer-burn
for love-bites.
I quite like lust,
mornings in bed,
salt on my tongue,
sweat. Red wrists.
I love to hear myself moaning.

Madonna

People who think
the world revolves around sex
bore me
unutterably.

Take last week.
I walk into a studio
full of Madonnas,
the original whore
lending her body out
to other people's purposes.

It's oppressive in here.
How those cow eyes stare.

Still, I feel sorry for her.
An immaculate conception –
oh, so squeaky clean –
I'll bet that was dull.
And He went to Hell before her.
What a wank.

Letter to a Friend (S.B.)

I found a squirrel floating
face down in Friendship
Park Pool today.
The fountain was shut,
like the roses, whose folds
clenched tight against the cold.

Autumn came to my window
in brazen mismatched colours.
So I put on beige shoes,
blood-red cotton –
my favourite summer dress,
the one you saw me in last –
to meet the chill
of a squirrel, swimming.

And just this morning,
I was thinking
(in my mirror)
that the mind is kind –
it won't understand death.

Doing the Dog

I was skating down the street today
to get my Guardian and pink toilet paper
when I saw this big old Alsatian dog
trying to eat its ass.

He reminded me of you.

'Cause I imagine that's what
you'd really like to do,
'cept you try to get me
to kiss yours instead.

Since that's not exactly my scene,
and this is my bed,
you can get out of it.

Now.

Voices

Sit under the lilac
in Friendship Park,
watch shadows emerge
with the sun,
listen to white-haired voices, brittle,
past blooming

until peace becomes tactile,
like damp earth
beneath grass
and the past
in that light
will seem benign.

Comment on a Candid Photograph

That picture was so cruel it was true.
You were looking in a mirror:
I was looking at you.

The Curse

So you're going to starve me to death,
chain me to this bed, let me lie in my shit
like a dog in the dark.
And you want to hear me beg.
Well, hear this:

May my brothers find you.
May my sisters dismember you.
May my cousins eat your eyes.
May my parents bury your tongue.
May my grandmother dice your ears.
May my aunts enjoy your wealth.
May my uncles erase all memory of you.
May my ancestor's ghosts destroy your soul.
May God have mercy on you:
we can't.

Meditation on Matisse Dancers

We heard the forest music:
followed; saw the dancers
rapt in leaves and clean sweat,
arms full out, bare
fingertips just touching
sky: flamingos' wings
stretched above a jungle
lake at twilight.

We were transported.
The drums beat the world
down, down, down.

We waited.
Demented worshippers
leapt into flame.

The circle opened.

Portrait in Dry Ice

And now I am glass.
Cut.
Fresh from the kiln,
blue as chilled toothpaste
but colder.
Pure.
Freed by fire,
the glow forever ground
into my veins,
in the skin.

And my heart is crystalline.

Don't be Black and Crazy in Britain

Honey, have you heard
about a bogus diagnosis
called cannabis psychosis?
If not, ask any British medic.
But I'll tell you a secret –
only black folks can get it.

Slice of Soweto

Police dumped him at my door tonight.
A pile for the Good-will to cart away,
bits and pieces,
the odd patch of blood
like day-old custard, dried.

I gathered him up,
rubbed my nose against his skin,
a new-born discovering smell.
I tried to recall his voice,
but, like music heard once
then never again,
he was gone.

Spring, Walking

I love the wind when it wrings
blossom showers from winter-weary trees,
or the sun, veiled like a good Muslim woman,
or the sound of children keeping quiet in church,
confused by the lack of joy round Easter-decked altars.

I am always a child at Easter,
sucking chocolate, crying for the Crucifixion
in every Jesus-movie ever made,
confessing what my soul can no longer retain,
brought to my knees by that need to be clean.
Life can do this, and more.

Driving Back From Durham

Bastille Day 1990

Suddenly it's summer in England.
Gilt sun on green water:
a yellow boat;
we four rowing raucously downriver.
We slip with the stream
under willow tress,
pulling leaves and laughing.
Our necks, backs, hands burned –
I wrung the water from my red dress
while my shoulders ached –
but the sun shone good,
and I was beginning
to look into your
sky eyes –
no, don't look, look down –
that was silly,
you'd think I was fourteen, not thirty –
but kindness is so seductive
and you are so kind.
I am beginning
as smiles tumble up streets,
we tumble up stairs
to tea and crumpets.
It could have been twee,
but not with these greedy people,
cramming down hot pie and cream.
The ride home was green,
and that hay on the side seemed
like blond blankets rolled –
God, it must be odd
to have gold hair.

I am beginning
for the first time in five years
to feel,
and fifty years on
I will close my eyes,
taste an apple pie,
a river,
cotton candy with flies,
and it will still be you.

The Coffee Bearer

oil painting by John Frederick Lewis, 1805-1876

Some old white man painted her
in a citrus-coloured gown,
her black velvet jacket
embroidered with birds of paradise,
to be heaven for a washed-up European.

The scene wallows in evening sun,
as if everyone in this village
could spend her days
singing, bowing, serving:
showing how shit-work
transmutes to joy.

She will be a toy,
brightly head-wrapped,
carrying cut-crystal vases
as clear as this portrait's lies.

I'll never serve anyone
with that smile in my eyes.

> (*'Painted after the artist's return from the Middle
> East, where he lived and painted for many years,
> adopting native dress and customs.'* –
> Manchester Art Galleries)

The Possibility of Fulfilment

As a child I believed
there was another part of me,
but he'd been born in China
and worked in a rice paddy,
while I was caught in DC.

Last night we were eating
(or at least he was – my food
kept slipping from my chopsticks).
We leaned so close together
(there was only one plate),
our cheeks touched.
Not for us the violation of tongues,
but touch, pure delight,
skin for skin alone,
known in dreams.

They make the day cold,
those memories.
I'm too old now
to learn Chinese.

Lemn Sissay

LEMN SISSAY lives in Manchester. He is Writers' Development Worker for Commonword, from which he created Cultureword, now the centre for black writers in the North West region. His first play, *Standing Speechless,* was performed at the Edinburgh Fringe in 1986, and his latest won the Black Theatre Forum's Playwrights Competition in 1989. He is co-founder of One Step Theatre Company.

He has performed his poetry throughout Great Britain and Europe, and has appeared many times on television and radio. He has published two collections: *Perceptions of the Pen* (1986) and *Tender Fingers in a Clenched Fist* (Bogle l'Ouverture 1988), and has produced several cassettes. His work appears in many national and international anthologies, including *New British Poetry* (Paladin 1989).

His first major collection is due from Bloodaxe Books in 1992.

A Black Man on the Isle of Wight

Faces cold as the stones stuck
to the sea's belly
with seaweed for hair
sculpted into expressions of fear.

Bearing Witness

(dedicated to James Baldwin who in his last
recorded interview said that he wanted black
writers to bear witness to the times)

Bearing witness to the times
where it pays to sell lines
where African thighs thrive for twenty five
and guns run with the midnight son.

Bearing witness to the days
of the blue eyed glaze
of the black eyed girl of the world
whose life depends on a contact lens .

Bearing witness to the screams
of children cut on shattered dreams,
colonialised minds lost in times
of permanent frowns and nervous breakdowns.

Bearing witness to the signs
of white sandstorms in black minds,
of waves from the west with white dagger crests
scratching the black beaches back.

Bearing witness to the hour
where maladjusted power
realigns its crimes in token signs
then perversely repents with self punishment.

Bearing witness to the times
where we black people define
the debt yet to be paid, you bet
I'll be rhyming the fact when I witness that.

Bearing Witness to be Free

I swear to speak the truth
the whole truth and nothing but the truth

so help me

Flowers in the Kitchen

On buying her flowers
she said

'There's no food in the kitchen
and we can't eat flowers'

On buying her food
she said

'You don't buy me flowers any more'

Suitcases and Muddy Parks

You say I am a lying child
I say   I'm not
you say there you go again

You say I am a rebellious child
I say no I'm not
you say there you go again

Quite frankly mum
I've never seen a rebellious child before
and when my mates said
jump in that puddle and race you through the park
(y'know, the muddy one)
I didn't think about the mud.

When you said why are you dirty!
I could feel the anger in your voice
I still don't know why.

I said I raced my mates through the park.
You said it was deliberate.
I said I didn't I mean I did but it wasn't.
You said I was lying,
I said no I am not.
You said there you go again.

Later in the dawn of adolescence
it was time for my leave
I with my suitcase, social worker,
you with your husband,
walked our sliced ways.

Sometimes I run back to you
like a child through a muddy park,
adult achievements tucked under my arm,
I explain them with a child-like twinkle,
thinking any mother would be proud . . .

Your eyes, desperately trying to be wise and unrevealing,
reveal all.
Still you fall back into the heart of the same rocking chair
saying There you go again.

And I did.

And I have.

Boiling Up

Can you spread me lightly on this street?
I would like to blend in.
If butter and bread can do it, so can I.

Will you sprinkle me softly in this hotel?
I would like to blend in.
If chicken and seasoning can do it, so can I.

(The store detective is either trying to
strike up some kind of meaningful relationship with me
or I've got a box of jelly babies stuck to my left ear.)

Could you drip me into this club?
I would like to blend in.
If coffee and milk can do it, so can I.

(It's not a sawn-off shotgun in my inside pocket,
and that's not because I keep my machete there –
ten Regal King size, please.)

Can you grate me into this city?
I would like to blend in.
If cheese and tomatoes can do it, so can I.

Can you soak me into this country?
I would like to blend in.
If rice and peas can do it, so can I.

Godsell

You knock upon my door
and open.
I drink to you.
This is a bad trip,
something about Armageddon
and pigs possessed by devils
flinging themselves from cliffs.
Look back into my house and I may turn to salt.

Blackened horizons itch with locusts,
whole pieces of earth slump
swallowed by the devil's breath;
Yea as I walk through the valley of death
with Lucifer in the crick of my back
an avalanche of commands befalls me
and I whimper from the cross and catapult
in the child's hand,
clutching a lock of my own hair,
feeling the heat of a burning bush
singe the back of my neck.
Three score and ten years of this;
look back and I may turn to salt.

Where is the chariot of fire
where is the chariot of fire
I, one piece of thirty pieces of silver,
a possessed pig, laugh at the cliff's edge,
snort and fling myself to the rocks.

When I meet Peter
I shall bribe him,
like I have been bribed.

The Customs Men

Breaking out from the plane
home's mouth lies wide open
from the white oesophagus corridors
guarded by the white English custom of suspicion,
and to prove my situation
I have written this so that

when they have fingered their
dirty hands through my clothes
mauled my enjoyable flight
with personal questions
pricked a little for reaction
and arrived at my book

I will point them to this poem
simply to tell them
that I get job satisfaction, in the end,
and they will get nothing but tobacco beneath their nails.

A Natural Woman

From the knots
  in a tree of fists
   in fits of rage
    to the
     sturdy presence
      where dewsweat curls down
       the inside of her neck branch
      into each morning.

     From the taut lips
   in each wave
  crying from deep
inside the whales' lost
orchestra,
Taut lips to kiss or bite the beaches back

From the eye
  of each Caribbean storm
   glaring at the loss of her whole self
    to be renamed Hugo and Gilbert and Jonathan
    glaring at the real Hugos and Gilberts
   who now lie skulking behind their own tombstones
  while she sweeps them clean
holding the storm in her eye.

Uncle Tom and the 1990's

The way he
bowed his head to the lilac princess,
spat on the young black boy

polished his shoes and ignored the news
of the lynching in his own backyard

or folded his clothes and held up his nose
to the sounds of a screaming sister:

Uncle Tom, the same syllable sound
as true or false, sweet and sour,
right or wrong, do or die,

is dead,
manacled mutated moaning in his grave
twisting and turning in all the suppressed unrest.

He sweeps the floors of hell
licks the walls of heaven
takes all the sinners to the pit of eternal fire:
children, crinkly old men, crimson young girls;
holds them by the hand, tells them
they'll be alright, they'll get used to it, and hums

'Oh lordy pick a bale of souls
Oh lordy pick a bale a day
gonna jump down turn around pick a bale of souls'

Everydoghasitsdayhewholivestorunawayifatfirstyoudont
succeedabirdinthehandisbettereyesbiggerthanyouranger
begetsangerdontrocktheboat

Frustrated black men still pull him from the grave

but the myth
has decomposed, doesn't hold together
the years between then and now.

We are at the crux of making
a martyr from a fool
a fool from a martyr.

Uncle Tom is dead.
Hot oil spittle pours from each orifice
his solidified words

Everycloudhasatheresgoodandbadinweareallthesameunder
liveandletlive

Make him a saint or a swearword,
both are a modern day charade.

There is no Uncle Tom in the '90's,
just cold black moving sculpture, sharp and sinister,
who know exactly what they're doing.

Fingerprints

I can see your fingerprints
fumbled all over this dead boy's body,
can see them in his
lifeless eyes,
in his fist clutched
by rigor mortis,
and holding up your hands to calm us people
you say: 'This was not a racial attack.'

I can see the wipe marks
on his forehead
where with the side of your fist
you tried to wipe them in

> smudge them in
> reshape them
> rub them in
> distort them
> change them
> hide them
> rearrange them

> with ink that dried
> before he died

You report

'We understand the victim was black.
This was not a racial attack.'

Rage

Take the sea in handfuls
and spill it onto this city's streets
and no one will notice at first
vagrants will laugh into the bottle
builders will point from the scaffolding
intellects will snort in mid-conversation
office workers will glance through windows.

Taking the sea in handfuls is not a loud task.
I may sing while I am doing it.
I may skip while carrying.
I am allowed.

The glances and snorts irritate.
'Yeah – it's the sea, ha!'
It feels so triumphant to let it
trickle through my fingers onto the cracked kerbs.

Love Poem

You remind me
define me
incline me

If you died
I'd

for my headstone

here is the death of the son you never had
the hand you never touched
the face you never stroked

here is the morning after
his bruises you never tended
the laughter you never shared

and here are the tears he'll never feel
your eyes he'll never see
whispers he'll never hear
the apologies
will squirm in his coffin
with the letters you never wrote

Acknowledgements

Debjani Chatterjee: *The London Delhi Poetry Quarterly; Iron; Yorkshire Television; Flame; Outposts;* Graves Art Gallery, Sheffield; *Artrage*
John Lyons: *Poetry Matters* 1988 & 1991
Cheryl Martin: *Identity* magazine

For full details of Smith/Doorstop Books, *The North* magazine, the Annual Competition and our Reading Service, send a stamped addressed envelope to: *The Poetry Business, 51 Byram Arcade, Westgate, Huddersfield HD1 1ND* (telephone 0484 434840 fax 0484 426566).